**DO YOU HAVE ANY IDEAS ON HOW TO
MAKE THE BOOK BETTER?
GET IN TOUCH!
LET'S IMPROVE THE BOOK TOGETHER.**

INFO@365-QUOTES.COM

- ARIANA GRANDE -

SINGER - SONGWRITER - ACTRESS

"I DO THINK MANIFESTATION IS REAL. IF YOU
WANT SOMETHING IT CAN HAPPEN, IT'S POSSIBLE."

- SHAWN MENDES -

SINGER - SONGWRITER - MUSICIAN

"I HAVE A BOOK OF MANIFESTATIONS. I DO BELIEVE
THAT IF YOU BREATH INTO THAT THING YOU WANT IN LIFE,
YOU WILL RECEIVE IT."

- KIM KARDASHIAN -

MEDIA PERSONALITY - BUSINESSWOMAN

"I HAVE A MANIFEST LIST.
MANIFESTATION IS ONE OF MY TALENTS."

- OPRAH WINFREY -

TALKSHOW HOST - ACTRESS - PRODUCER

"I'AM A POWERFUL MANIFESTER."

- BELLA POARCH -

SOCIAL MEDIA PERSONALITY

USES MANIFESTATION REGULARLY.
SHE HAS A SIMPLE MANIFESTATION PROCESS
AND HIS OWN MANIFESTATION RULES.

- STEVE HARVEY -

TV HOST - COMEDIAN - ACTOR

"IF YOU SEE IT IN YOUR MIND,
YOU CAN HOLD IT IN YOUR HAND."

- DRAKE -

RAPPER - SONGWRITER - ENTREPRENEUR

"I FEEL THAT THINGS THAT I REPETITIVELY THINK ABOUT
OR SAY I'M ABLE TO MANIFEST. LIKE THIS HOUSE
FOR EXAMPLE, I MANIFESTED THIS."

- POST MALONE -

RAPPER - SINGER - SONGWRITER

"IF YOU WANT TO ACHIEVE SOMETHING, IF YOU WANT TO
DO SOMETHING, YOU GOT TO SPEAK IT INTO EXISTENCE.
KEEP TALKING ABOUT IT, KEEP BELIEVING IN YOURSELF."

- JENNIFER LOPEZ -

SINGER - ACTRESS

"I'AM OPEN AND RECEPTIVE TO ALL THE GOODNESS
AND ABUNDANCE THE UNIVERSE HAS TO OFFER."

- JIM CARREY -

ACTOR - COMEDIAN

"YES, I BELIEVE IN MANIFESTATION. YOU GET IT
WHEN YOU BELIEVE YOU HAVE IT. THAT'S THE KEY."

- ASHLEY GRAHAM -

SINGER MODEL - TV PRESENTER

"SPEAK WHAT YOU WANT, MAKE IT YOUR TRUTH
AND IT WILL COME TRUE."

- CONOR MCGREGOR -

MULTIPLE MMA WORLD CHAMPION

"IF YOU CAN SEE IT IN YOUR MIND AND
HAVE THE COURAGE TO SPEAK IT, IT WILL HAPPEN."

Your Free Gift

As a way of saying thanks for your purchase, I'm offering the book "30-Day Happiness Challenge: Proven Techniques For a Life Full of Joy, Happiness & Self-Love – Become a Happier Person in As Little As 30 Days" for **FREE** to my readers.

To get instant access just go to:

www.tomas.coach/free-gift-1

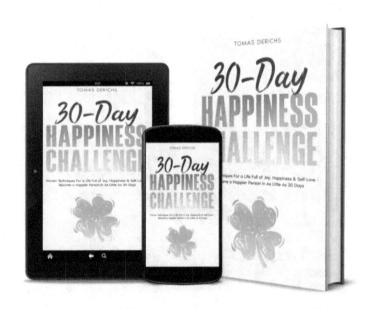

Inside the book, you will discover:

- **How 30 days** can transform your life into one of lasting happiness.

- **Proven techniques** that instantly boost your joy and well-being.

- **5-minute tasks with** the potential for profound effects on your life.

- **And so much more!** All designed to easily fit into your busy life.

If you want to experience a happier life full of endless joy and deep self-love for yourself and your loved ones, make sure to grab the free book.

Get Your Gift!

If you want to experience a happier life full of endless joy and deep self-love for yourself and your loved ones, make sure to grab the free book.

SCAN ME

Inside the book, you will discover:

- **How 30 days** can transform your life into one of lasting happiness.

- **Proven techniques** that instantly boost your joy and well-being.

- **5-minute tasks with** the potential for profound effects on your life.

- **And so much more!** All designed to easily fit into your busy life.

MAKE THIS DAY GREAT!

THE FUTURE STARTS TODAY

I WILL MAKE IT!

I GOT THIS

DO
THE SMALL
STEPS
EVERY DAY

NO ACTION
NO CHANGES

PUNCH
YOUR FEAR
IN THE
FACE

MY POTENTIAL
IS LIMITLESS

EVERY DOLLLAR
I SPEND AND INVEST
COMES BACK
TO ME MULTIPLIED

I WILL DO
BIG THINGS!

HOW BIG
WOULD YOU DREAM,
IF YOU KNEW
YOU COULDN'T FAIL

STAY
FOCUSED

CREATE
YOUR FUTURE!

BE PATIENT
NOTHING IN NATURE
BLOOMS ALL YEAR.

A MOMEMT
OF PAIN FOR A
LIFETIME OF GLORY

Your Free Gift

As a way of saying thanks for your purchase, I'm offering the book "30-Day Happiness Challenge: Proven Techniques For a Life Full of Joy, Happiness & Self-Love – Become a Happier Person in As Little As 30 Days" for **FREE** to my readers.

To get instant access just go to:

www.tomas.coach/free-gift-1

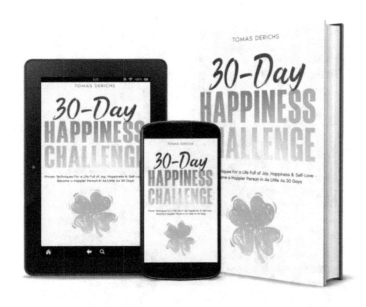

Inside the book, you will discover:

- **How 30 days** can transform your life into one of lasting happiness.

- **Proven techniques** that instantly boost your joy and well-being.

- **5-minute tasks with** the potential for profound effects on your life.

- **And so much more!** All designed to easily fit into your busy life.

If you want to experience a happier life full of endless joy and deep self-love for yourself and your loved ones, make sure to grab the free book.

Get Your Gift!

If you want to experience a happier life full of endless joy and deep self-love for yourself and your loved ones, make sure to grab the free book.

SCAN ME

Inside the book, you will discover:

- **How 30 days** can transform your life into one of lasting happiness.

- **Proven techniques** that instantly boost your joy and well-being.

- **5-minute tasks with** the potential for profound effects on your life.

- **And so much more!** All designed to easily fit into your busy life.

Your Feedback Matters!

So please write me a review.

It will only take 30 seconds
and will allow me to keep
publishing quality books.

Made in the USA
Las Vegas, NV
02 January 2025

15691771R00059